Organic Gardens

Beginners Guide To Growing Healthy Organic Gardens

TOM FORD

COPYRIGHT © 2014

ALL RIGHTS RESERVED

Disclaimer

No part of this eBook can be transmitted or reproduced in any form including print, electronic, photocopying, scanning, mechanical or recording without prior written permission from the author.

While the author has taken utmost efforts to ensure the accuracy of the written content, all readers are advised to follow the information mentioned herein at their own risk. The author cannot be held responsible for any personal or commercial damage caused by misinterpretation of information.

All ideas, views and thoughts expressed in this eBook are the author's own. References have been provided wherever possible. *Organic Vertical Gardens* is not affiliated, authorized or endorsed with any of the brands and names mentioned in here unless specified otherwise. This book is not meant for promotional or advertising purposes.

All information contained here is meant to be taken as a guideline. The gardening experience can be different from person to person owing to different climates; soil types, plant availability etc and the advice contained herein is mentioned in a neutral manner. It is understood that the reader claims responsibility for their own actions.

The author does not claim nor was any guarantee made regarding any success through this book. Therefore they cannot be held responsible should any losses, risks, liabilities or damages occur, that might be linked, directly or indirectly, with the information contained within this book.

Table of Contents

Introduction 8

What Is Vertical Gardening? 10

    Mat Media 12

    Loose Media 13

    Structural media 14

Why Build Vertical Gardens? 15

Supplies and Tools Needed 20

    Vertical Planters 21

    Plants 22

    Soil 23

    Gardening Equipment 24

Outdoor vs Indoor Vertical Gardens 26

    Indoor Gardens 27

    Outdoor Gardens 32

Preparing the Soil 37

    Different Soils & Their Benefits 39

        Sand: 39

Peat moss: 39

Manure: 39

Lime: 39

Leaf mold: 39

Compost: 40

Ground bark: 40

Topsoil: 40

Fertilizers 41

Making The Best Organic Compost 42

Tools You Will Need 43

Directions 44

Growing Vegetable & Fruits 47

Maintenance 53

Location 53

Nutrients & Water 54

Tending To Plants 55

Irrigation Systems for Vertical Gardens 56

Drip Irrigation System – Gravity Fed 57

Drip Irrigation System – Comprehensive 58

Pipe Network 59

Pest Control 60

- Common Pests & How to Control Them 61
  - Aphids 61
  - Caterpillars 62
  - Cutworms 63
  - Mexican Bean Beetle 64
  - Flea Beetles 65
- **Keeping Your Vertical Garden Healthy** 66
  - Common Plant Diseases & Their Prevention 67
    - Alternaria Blight 67
    - Bacterial Blight 68
    - Rots 69
    - Verticillium & Fusarium Wilt 69
    - Downy Mildew 70
- **Making Vertical Gardening Fun!** 71
  - Boot Planters 72
  - Vertical Towers 73
  - Using Frames 74
- ****BONUS: Examples of Vertical Gardens** 76
- **Conclusion** 80
- **About The Author** 81
- **Check Out These Books** 82

Introduction

When we hear the word "Garden" our mind automatically comes up with an image of lush green grass, tall trees, and a bed of flowers, but did you know that, you can actually grow gardens on a wall?

Crazy concept, I know. But yes, it's true. And yes, it is very much possible to do!

Vertically gardening is a fairly old concept but it has recently started getting popular. They are also called green walls as it is quite simply a wall or a free standing structure covered entirely or partially in plants. They are a perfect solution for urban areas where there are less open spaces and therefore less room for gardening.

People can now have their own green walls right inside their living rooms or on their balconies in no time.

Vertical gardens is also a dream come true for people who want to grow their own produce, rather than buying them at a market, but cannot do so because of limited space. With the help of vertical gardening you can now grow your favorite vegetables inside the comfort of your own home.

Don't worry even if you are new to gardening and don't know much about it. This book is a beginner's guide and we will walk you every step of the way and by the time you finish reading the book you will have your own green wall.

Let's get started!

What Is Vertical Gardening?

Vertical gardening is one of the oldest techniques of gardening but it was not until recently that it started becoming a trend.

It involves employing various resources to facilitate plants to grow upwards rather than growing on a horizontal platform.

Some plants do not require any support of trellis or fences to grow upwards such as ivy, while there are some fruits and vegetables that require support of trellises, cages, and stakes in order to extend upwards.

Green walls, another name for vertical gardens, are a surging trend in urban cities.

Vertical gardens are not only pleasing to the eyes and add a lot of elegance to a space but they are also a perfect solution to maintain a favorable temperature inside a building.

In bigger cities heat builds ups and increases the temperature inside closed spaces, the major cause of this is insulation, which means the absorption of heat by building materials.

However, due to the process of transpiration the temperature of plant surfaces do not rise more than 4 to 5 degree Centigrade above the surroundings.

Vertical gardens are of three types categorized on the basis of the growth media used to plant them:

1. **Mat media**
2. **Loose media**
3. **Structural media**

Mat Media

Mat media is often felt mats or coir fiber.

It tends to be thin even if you place them in multiple layers and therefore might not support mature roots for more than 3 to 5 years.

Mat media is best for plants that do not mature to weight that can rip off the mat or in indoor areas where seismic activity is low. They are also suitable for installations that are not taller than 8 feet in height so that damages can be repaired easily.

Loose Media

Loose media is durable for a longer period of time and require low maintenance.

It is "soil-in-a-bag" kind of system where soil in placed in small bags and then place on the walls, fences, or trellises.

This system needs soil replacement once in every two years indoors, and once every year outdoors.

Structural media

This is the best combination of mat and loose media and consists of blocks that can be made in various thicknesses, shapes, and sizes.

These blocks are durable for as long as ten to fifteen years and are easy to replace and maintain.

Now that we know what vertical gardening is and what are its various types, we will now be discussing its benefits in detail.

Why Build Vertical Gardens?

There are endless benefits of building vertical gardens. Not only are they visually appealing but there are a number of ecological reasons why we should plant them.

We all know that plants clean the air we breathe in by absorbing the air pollutants. Even a 50 square feet patch of a vertical garden is enough to consume as much CO_2 from air as a 14' high tree.

But this is not it; following are some of the major benefits of building vertical gardens.

Reduction in Carbon Emission

Vertical gardens also known as green walls lower the cooling and heating costs because it keeps the walls cooler in summers and warm in winters, hence reducing the amount of carbon emitted by air conditioners or heaters.

Green walls also absorb, disperse, and deflect the rays of the sun lowering the overall air temperature.

Noise Pollution

Green walls cause noise attenuation resulting in quieter streets and buildings giving us a more peaceful and stress free environment.

Air Purification

Plants filter the air we breathe in by absorbing the pollutants in air especially if they are placed inside.

Research shows that plants cleanse the air of harmful toxic chemicals that are commonly found in buildings such as Formaldehyde, Xylene, Toluene, Benzene, TCO, CO, and VOCs.

Decrease Stress

Flowers and foliage in the surrounding environment improve human health by relieving mental stress.

Space

Planting vertical gardens give you more space to move around especially if you have limited space.

You can place trellises or fences in a way that not only conserves space but also allow you to plant a wide variety of vegetables, plants, or flowers even in a tiny space.

Ambiance

Planting gardens vertically allows you to build structures like gazebos, pergolas, arches, and arbors that adds a lot to the aesthetics of your house.

You can decorate the entrances of your house and gardens giving them a grand look; not only that but having a vertical garden structure can add depth to a small space.

Accessibility

Vertical plant are make harvesting, pruning, watering, and fertilizing much more easily than horizontal gardens.

They are easier to reach and also do not strain your back which may be caused by tending to horizontal gardens.

Plant Health

Plants that are growing upwards have improved air circulation which results in less plant diseases and pest problems.

Vertical gardens are less prone to damage caused by wild animals or pets digging up the horizontal garden.

Variety of Plants

Since vertical gardens gives you more space to work in, you can plant more plants even within a tiny space.

Vegetables such as pumpkin can take a lot of space, but they can be urged to grow upwards on a fence or a trellis even in limited space.

Supplies and Tools Needed

The supplies and tools that you need for planting a vertical garden depends largely upon the medium that you choose, plants that you grow, and the design that you want to build.

Following are some of the basic tools and supplies that you would need in order to build a vertical garden.

Let's take a look..

Vertical Planters

There are many options available of planters that you can choose from depending on the type of plant that you want to grow.

Following are the four most common types of planters used in vertical gardening:

1. Towers
2. Recycled containers
3. Pockets
4. Pots

Out of these four options pockets are the easiest to work with as they are ideal if you are working in a small space.

Pots add versatility to the overall design but they may require installation of additional framing for support. Using recycled material is always a good choice because it is also eco friendly.

Plants

Grass, herbs, flowering plants, and vegetables are some of the most commonly grown plants in vertical gardens.

Before buying plants for your garden consider the purpose of planting a vertical garden in the first place. If you want to build a living wall then leafy plants or grass is the best choice.

If you are building the vertical garden in your kitchen then planting herbs would be more feasible. If your aim is to increase the aesthetic appeal of your house then you can grow flowering plants to give your house a decorative touch.

Knowing the purpose of your garden is the easiest way to choose a plant. If you are a professional gardener then you can even grow a combination of plants on a single wall.

Soil

The choice of soil largely depends upon the plant that you choose to grow because different types of plants require different types of soil or plotting material.

All plants grow well in fertile soil but some plants thrive better when they are planted in a special combination of potting mixes.

If you are new at gardening then consult a professional gardener before buying soil or any other plotting material.

Gardening Equipment

After you have decided on what plant to grow and plotting material suitable for that plant, the next step is to buy the basic gardening equipment.

1. Watering plants regularly is very important but in case you cannot use a watering hose inside then a watering can is the next best option. We will be discussing more about the irrigation system for vertical gardens in the upcoming chapters.

2. You will need a trowel for weeding.

3. If you are building a vertical garden inside your house where plants may not get sufficient sunlight then you will have to buy lamps and lights to make up for it.

4. You will also need various hand tools such as scissors and rakes to tend to the plants.

5. Fungicides, pesticides, and insect killers will also be needed to save your plants from being destroyed by insects, pests and various plant diseases.

Garden supplies that you might need also depends on the plants that you opt to grow. You can easily find garden supplies in any local gardening shop or in an online store.

Now that we have discussed the tools and supplies needed to put up a vertical garden, we will compare the pros and cons of outdoor and indoor vertical gardens in detail.

Outdoor vs Indoor Vertical Gardens

Vertical gardens not only give you more room to grow plants but they are also a work of art and can add a lot to the ambiance of your house.

In today's age when you can no longer be sure about the nutritional value of the produce that you buy from the market, being able to grow your own vegetables even in limited space is nothing less than a dream come true.

The location of the vertical garden is as important as the medium and tools you use to grow it. In this chapter we will elaborately compare outdoor and indoor vertical gardens and the pros and cons of each.

Indoor Gardens

Vertical gardens also known as living walls can be grown anywhere inside a building.

PRO'S OF INDOOR GARDENS

Following are some of the advantages of planting an indoor vertical garden.

Quality of Air

Foliage and plants can greatly improve the quality of the air that you breathe in. Plants are natural air filters as they absorb the pollutants from the air while releasing oxygen.

Installing a vertical garden inside an office building can increase the productivity of the employees and enhance their health. Fresh and clean air leads to better concentration and a stress free working environment.

Ambiance

An indoor living wall, be it inside a house or an office can give life to a dreary and dull surrounding.

It adds a very refreshing element to the environment and can create a great first impression on your guests or business clients.

Planting flowers in an indoor vertical garden can add a lot of color in an otherwise dull four walled room.

Energy Costs

Cost of air conditioning can be astronomically high. However, a living wall can serve the same purpose of an air conditioner because it cools the air naturally and also balances the humidity in the environment with a process known as evapotranspiration.

Noise

This might come as a little shock but living walls can greatly reduce the loud background noises by reflecting noise that comes its way.

Not only that but it also adds a general sense of calm and tranquility to the surroundings that comes naturally by being around greenery.

CON'S OF INDOOR GARDENS

Now that we have discussed the advantages of indoor vertical gardens, following are some of its drawbacks.

Limited Growing Space

The planters used in growing plants in vertical garden do not provide a lot of space for the roots to grow.

Unless heavy duty planters are used the large plants cannot be supported. This might limit the gardener to work only with smaller and slower growing plants.

Cost

Planters used in vertical gardens costs more than traditional gardening pots. These pre-made vertical planting structures for vertical gardens easy maintenance and watering.

However, you can also make your own structures using less materials and money.

High Maintenance

An indoor vertical garden requires high maintenance. Dirt can fall out of the vertical planters, and water might leak, creating a mess on the living room floor.

The water can also damage the wall or the support structure. Drainage of water might also be an issue.

Outdoor Gardens

With an ever increasing pollution in the urban areas, vertical gardening is the best solution to increasing the greenery in the environment and to curb the air pollution or at least build your own little space where you can breathe in fresh and clean air.

PRO'S OF OUTDOOR GARDENS

Following are some of the major advantages of outdoor vertical gardening.

Protects the Building

A living wall on the outside of not only makes the building look more beautiful and aesthetically appealing but it can also extend the life of the building exterior by shielding it from the harmful UV rays and heavy hail or rain.

Heat Energy

In cold weathers an outdoor living walls can naturally heat the inside environment by a process of insulation reducing the need and cost of a heater.

Water Conservation

Vertical gardening uses much less water than traditional farming practices. It also saves the water from being wasted.

The excess water is accumulated in a drainage tray at the base of the vertical garden from where it can be drained away or recycled and reused to water the plants.

Few Pests

As the plants grow upwards many pests cannot even reach the plants upwards which mean that vertical gardens use less insecticides and pesticides.

They get better sunlight therefore the chances of diseases and fungus are greatly reduced.

Less Spoilage

Since the produce from the vertical gardens can be used just after they are harvested, the margin of wasted produce is much less.

Plus there is no transportation cost because the produced vegetable cost can be used within the city.

CON'S OF OUTDOOR GARDENS

Following are some of the disadvantages of outdoor vertical gardens.

Can Dry Quickly

Outdoor vertical gardens are more exposed to the sun and can dry quickly which might weakens or kills the plant.

Therefore it is important that you pick the material carefully when building a planter for the living walls.

Limited Variety of Plants

Large plants and vegetables need more stable planters that can be a little more costly.

This leaves a small variety of plants and vegetables that can be grown in a vertical system. However this problem can be overcome by using high quality planters that can take the weight of a large plant and have enough room for the roots to grow.

This was the comparison of indoor and outdoor vertical gardens at a glance. The advantages of vertical gardens be it inside or outside your house or office building outranks the drawbacks.

The drawbacks can be eliminated by proper planning and maintenance of the plants, more on which will be discussed in the upcoming chapters.

Preparing the Soil

This is the most important step in planting a garden.

Soil is like the soul of garden and without it the garden will not flourish. The first thing that you need to know when preparing the soil is to know its type. Remember that soil is not synonymous with dirt.

You can expect to just throw the seeds and expect them to grow on their own. In order to grow healthy plants the soil need to be rich in nutrients to allow the plants to absorb nutrition, anchor roots, and grow strong.

There is more than one way testing the soil. You can buy a do-it-yourself kit from a local garden store, or you can send the sample of the soil to a lab for testing.

When planting a vertical garden you can buy prepared soil that has been tested and is rich in nutrients. You can also prepare your own soil by composting, more on which will be discussed in the second part of this chapter.

If you don't have ideal soil then you can fix it by using any one of the following methods:

1. Add peat moss, compost, and coarse sand to fix clay soil.
2. Add sawdust with more nitrogen, aged manure or humus to fix sandy soil. Clay rich soil can also be added to sandy soil to improve its quality.
3. Add rotted horse manure combined with straw, compost, gravel, and coarse sand to fix silt soil.

Different Soils & Their Benefits

These are the different types of soils:

Sand: Enhances the drainage of clay soil.

Peat moss: Functions as a conditioner and help the soil in retaining water.

Manure: It is best when rotted and composted. Also functions as a conditioner.

Lime: Is used in acidic soil o increase it pH and also helps in loosening clay soil.

Leaf mold: These are decomposed leaves that add structure and nutrients to the soil.

Compost: It is an excellent conditioner.

Ground bark: It is a mixture of various barks of trees and also enhances the structure of soil.

Topsoil: It is usually used along another soil and is used to replace the existing soil.

The soil that you use when planting a vertical garden depends a lot on the type of plant that you want to grow.

If you are just a beginner and don't know much about gardening and soils then you can take advice from a professional gardener about which soil depending in the plant that you want to grow.

Fertilizers

Once you are clear about the kind of soil that is perfect for the type of plants that you want to grow, the next most important thing is the choice of the fertilizer.

Here are some common choices:

1. **Nitrogen (N)** makes plants greener and is suitable for the growth of leaves.
2. **Phosphorus (P)** is best for the production of fruits and the growth of a strong root.
3. **Potassium (K)** helps the plant to fight the diseases and stay healthy.

Making The Best Organic Compost

Organic vertical gardeners use rich organic matter as the foundation of their gardens to maintain the high quality of the soil.

Some gardeners make their own compost by recycling the waste. As a beginner you can also make your own compost from the waste from your kitchen and make healthy compost to plant your organic vertical garden.

Following is a simple method of preparing the perfect solid compost for the vertical garden.

Tools You Will Need

1. **Shovel/ Garden fork**
2. **Grill**
3. **Wood/ Plastic bin**

Directions

1. Take a 20 gallon wood or plastic bin and drill holes in it on all sides to allow the circulation of air. Make sure that you place the bin in a protected and warm location. Do not leave it outside in the sun or where it can be exposed to rain as these elements will destroy the compost.

2. To give structure to the compost, fill one quarter of the bin with soil. Then add organic kitchen waste such as nuts, scraps of fruits, coffee ground, egg shells, bread and scraps of vegetables.

3. To create a balance between kitchen scraps that are rich in nitrogen and garden scraps that are rich in carbon, add straw, manure, wood, grass and leaves in it. Add paper waste such as tissue, papers and cardboard. You can use a wide variety of ingredients to make healthy and nutrient rich compost.

4. Add water in the bin until the ingredients are moist but not soggy. Consistent moisture is required for the content to breakdown. Be careful not to over water. The compost.

5. Stir the compost at least twice a day with the help of a shovel. The microorganism breaking down the ingredients need adequate air therefore shuffling the ingredients will speed of the composting process.

6. You can add more ingredients in the compost every once in a week. Not only making your compost is a cheaper option but it also helps you in getting rid of the waste in a more productive way. Add adequate moisture to keep the ingredients moist.

7. You can use the compost to plant your vertical garden once it is dark uniformly and a crumbly

consistency. Take the dark portion only and leave the unfinished ingredients in the bin for the process to complete.

Now that you know the basics about preparing the soil and making organic compost, it is time to move on to the ideal organic vegetables and fruits that you can grow in your vertical garden.

Growing Vegetable & Fruits

In this section we will discuss the best organic fruits and vegetables that are ideal for vertical spaces and can easily grow upwards.

Strawberries

Strawberries have shallow roots that allow them to grow upwards by taking hold of the vertical spaces which makes them an ideal choice or an organic vertical garden.

You can also grow them in a gutter garden or a PVC pipe which is drilled with holes and filled with soil. Strawberry plants need around 7 to 8 hours of sunlight to grow therefore they need to grow in a spot with sufficient sunlight.

Cherry Tomatoes

These are a type of small tomatoes and are vine based which makes them a perfect choice for a vertical garden. Like normal tomatoes they need ample sunlight and attention.

Plant them in a loose and well fertilized soil and water them regularly. If you are using seeds instead of seedlings then it is important that you plant them early enough to provide them with at least 2 to 3 months of warm weather.

Their need for light and heat makes them a perfect plant to be grown in balconies or walls under direct sunlight for most part of the day.

Cucumbers

All varieties of cucumbers are grown on vines so you can choose any type of cucumber to grow in your vertical garden.

If you are planting cucumbers in a container garden then choose a dwarf variety.

Plant cucumbers against a fence or a trellis and then gently weave the vines on the surface as they grow.

If you want to grow a full size cucumber then tie a stretchy piece of cloth between the fruit and the fence, this will give the fruit the required support and allow it to grow strong.

Beans

There are many varieties in beans that need a surface to grow upward such as pole beans. The small tendrils sprouting from the vines of pole beans grasp the vertical surface as they grow.

The best support for tendril type plants are tepee or trellis made of thin poles. All types of beans need ample supply of water therefore make sure that you water the bean plants regularly.

Legumes

Peas and green beans both do not need vertical support to grow but they have some varieties that van grow on a fence or a trellis. Peas produce more fruits if they are grown on a pole rather than a bush.

You will have to place poles and wires to assist the plant to grow vertically. A tepee made of bamboos is a perfect support for beans and peas.

Leafy Vegetables

Leafy vegetables have a compact form and shallow roots. They will not climb a trellis or a fence but they make a perfect choice for garden pockets.

Garden pockets are pockets filled with soil with a plant placed in each pocket. Kale, spinach, broccoli, and Lettuce can be grown in garden pockets.

Radishes

Edible roots require a lot of room and soil depth to grow with an exception of old radish which grows perfectly cramped quarters.

The depth of the seed will determine the size of the radish, the most important thing to consider when planting a radish is the quality of the soil.

They grow best in sandy loam and under ample sunlight.

Tomatoes

You can grow tomatoes in your vertical garden in a staking or a wire cage. If you are sowing the seed directly in the soil then the caging method is the best option.

To make a cage take a 5X6 foot piece of support wire and place it around the plant. Push the cage a little in the ground to save it from blowing away in strong winds. Since the plant is supported from all sides tying will not be needed for additional support.

Now that you are aware of the vegetables and fruits that you can grow in your vertical garden the next thing to learn is its maintenance.

Maintenance

Vertical gardens are ideal especially for people who are living in urban areas and have less room to grow a traditional garden.

Plants cultivated in vertical gardens needs to be trained to grow upwards and therefore needs regular maintenance. Tending to a vertical garden is not as hard as it sounds; following are some tips that will you take care and maintain the vertical garden.

Location

One of the most important factors in maintaining the health of a vertical garden is the location of it.

Like all plants, the plants grown in vertical gardens also require ample sunlight and therefore the garden should be placed in a location where the plants can get the required sunlight.

If you have an indoor vertical garden then artificial light should be placed to give the plants required heat and light to grow into healthy, strong plants.

Nutrients & Water

The plants that are sown in vertical gardens use very limited soil and therefore you need to add the required nutrients in water.

To deliver nutrient rich water to the plants you can place a gravity fed system of irrigation.

The irrigation system will make sure that the water reaches all the plants regularly all you have to do in terms of maintenance is to make sure that water drippers function properly without any blockages and that the plants are getting balanced nutrition.

Tending To Plants

Regardless of the type of plant you choose to grow in your garden, all of them require particular care.

Another important thing about growing plants in a vertical garden is to train them to grow upwards otherwise they might start growing in a haphazard and unmanageable manner.

In order to make them grow upwards you can trim them without disturbing the roots to make them grow in a particular direction. When the plants are old enough you might want to add more support to the structure such as using twine to tying up the plants.

Irrigation Systems for Vertical Gardens

Like traditional gardens the key to growing vertical gardens is a proper irrigation system.

Without regular supply of water the plants will start to dry up and die. Since vertical gardens are placed on walls, therefore they are more exposed to sunlight and need adequate water supply to save them from drying up.

Following are some of the three most commonly used irrigation systems used to water vertical gardens:

1. **Drip Irrigation System – Gravity Fed**
2. **Drip Irrigation System – Comprehensive**
3. **Pipe Network**

Drip Irrigation System – Gravity Fed

In this system a traditional drip is placed at the top of the vertical garden and water is released in it which drips down to the first row of the plants.

Once the top row of plants get sufficient water the water starts to travel down to other rows through the effect of gravity.

The excess water accumulates at the base of the garden and can be drained away or a pump can be installed to recycle and reuse the water.

Drip Irrigation System - Comprehensive

In case the plants that you choose to grow require more water, then a comprehensive irrigation system is a better choice.

In this system you can install irrigation lines in each row to supply sufficient water to each plant separately.

This system also the water is accumulated at the base of the vertical garden and can be recycled or drained.

Pipe Network

A pipe network can also be used to water the vertical garden.

In this system perforated pipes are arranged in a network through the entire vertical garden. Water rich in nutrients is released in these pipes at regular intervals and it is then carried to the plants.

The intervals of releasing water can be controlled by a timer so you don't have to worry about watering the plants again and again. This system is used for gardens that use less soil and is more of a hydroponics method of irrigation.

Pest Control

In this chapter we will be discussing some of the most common pests that might threaten the health of your plants and the ways in which you can prevent them from ruining the plants in your vertical garden.

We'll look at:

- **Common Pests & How to Control Them**
- **Aphids**
- **Caterpillars**
- **Cutworms**
- **Mexican Bean Beetle**
- **Flea Beetles**

Common Pests & How to Control Them

The threat of pest infestation in vertical gardens is less than that in traditional gardens and farms but it is there nonetheless and therefore you need to take care of it before your hard work goes to waste.

Following are the most common pests and the ways in which you can eradicate them.

Aphids

These are small pear shaped insects, with long antennas and two tube like structures going rearward through abdomen. They are commonly found in vegetables, fruits and flowers.

Damage

They suck the plant sap which damages the foliage and causes the leaves to drop. They also excrete honeydew on leaves of the plants which supports the growth of sooty mold and encourages viral plant diseases.

Control

Apply garlic repellents or hot pepper on plants or wash them with a strong stream of water to remove the pests. If the problem becomes severe and persists then apply neem, insecticidal soap or horticulture soil.

Caterpillars

These are soft larvae with a distinct capsule. They have six legs in front and false flashy legs on the rear. They are most commonly found in shade trees, ornamentals, fruits and vegetables.

Damage

They chew on leaves and fruits and make tunnels into them making them unfit for consumption.

Control

Spray with spinosod or Bacillus Thuringiensis, or apply a cover on rows of plants, hand pick them, or encourage native parasites of predators.

Cutworms

They are fat larvae and around an inch in length with black segmented bodies. They are usually active at night. They are most commonly found in flower seedlings and vegetables.

Damage

These are most damaging during May and June and they chew through the roots and leaves and might completely eat the small plants.

Control

You can hand pick them or use cutworm collars. You can also scatter bran baits combined with B.t. var. kurstaki and molasses in soil before sowing the seeds.

Mexican Bean Beetle

The larvae of Mexican bean beetle are dark yellow and fat with grubs, branched and long spines. The adults are yellow-brown and oval in shape about ¼ inches in size and have 16 black spots on the cover of wings. They can infest soybeans, snap beans, lima beans, and cowpeas.

Damage

Both larvae and the adult eat the leave from beneath leaving them with a lacy appearance. They cause the plant to defoliate and then eventually die.

Control

Spray the plant with neem, insecticidal soap, or Beauveria bassiana.

Flea Beetles

They are dark and small and jump like fleas when disturbed. They can infest most of the vegetable crops.

Damage

These are most damaging to young plants. The adults chew holes in the leaves and the larvae attacks the roots of the plants.

Control

This flea can be repelled by spraying kaolin clay or garlic spray on the plant if the infestation becomes severe then spray with spinsod or Beauveria bassina.

Keeping Your Vertical Garden Healthy

Apart from pest infestation another threat to the plants are various plant diseases. In this chapter we will discuss common diseases in plants along with ways and methods to prevent them.

- **Alternaria Blight**
- **Bacterial Blight**
- **Rots**
- **Verticillium & Fusarium Wilt**
- **Downy Mildew**

Common Plant Diseases & Their Prevention

Your plants are under a constant threat of pests and plant diseases and therefore they need you regular care and attention.

Following are some of the common diseases that can ruin the plants in your vertical garden.

Alternaria Blight

This disease infects fruits, vegetables and ornamental plants. When it appears on peppers, potatoes, or tomatoes it is called early blight.

In this disease black to brown spots spear on leaves and they enlarge. Heavily spotted leaves eventually die. In a tomato plant target like spots appear.

Control

To prevent the disease promote good air circulation in plants. Apply Trichoderma harzianum to the soil before you sow the seeds.

Bacterial Blight

This disease is most commonly found in legumes. Foliage infected with this disease exhibit water soaked spots they eventually drop out after drying. Lesions occur on stems that are dark and long. Spots may also ooze slime.

Control

Remove the plant that has been infected. Avoid touching the plants when they are wet as that might spread the disease.

Rots

This disease cause decay of fruit, flowers, woods, stems, and roots. Rots can be squishy and soft or dry and hard depending upon the type of disease. The disease is usually caused by fungi and bacteria.

Control

To prevent the disease keep the soil well drained.

Verticillium & Fusarium Wilt

These are fungal wilts that might attack ornamentals, fruits, vegetables, and flowers. This causes the plant to wilt and turn yellow.

Control

Cut off the parts that show the symptoms of wilt to prevent the disease from spreading.

Downy Mildew

This is a fungal disease that attacks grasses, flowers, vegetables, and fruits. The initial symptom of the disease is downy growth, white-purple usually along stems and under the leaves and they become black with age.

Eventually the top of the leaves turn pale and as the disease progresses it overwinters the infected areas but the viable parts of the plants can grow. This disease is spread by rain, winds or in seeds.

Control

The basic thing is to buy seeds that are free of this disease. Remove the infected part of the plants and use preventive sprays.

Making Vertical Gardening Fun!

Vertical gardening is more than just a plank of wood, a fence or a trellis on which you grow a bunch of plants.

You can make this activity a lot more fun by adopting various ideas. It is not necessary that you plant a vertical garden on a straight wall in a non-fun way. Rather you can make it colorful and engaging.

In this section we will discuss different ideas which will make gardening interesting rather than a tedious job and not only will it allow you to grow plants of your choice but it will also allow you to do so in a very unique and engaging manner.

Here are some creative ways to make gardening more fun.

Boot Planters

Do you find pockets boring? Use the boot planters on your walls to grow your favorite flowers.

Vertical Towers

Tired of growing plants on a straight wall? Buy a tower or build one to add fun and color in your gardening routine.

Using Frames

Grow plants inside a frame because pots and walls are just too mainstream. Build your own green frame.

You can make use of any of these ideas or add life to your vertical garden by bringing in your creativity. There is just no limit to the fun that you can add to your gardening just by becoming a little creative.

Add colors to your walls and add life to your house inside and out!

**BONUS: Examples of Vertical Gardens

Following are some more examples that you can use as a source of inspiration to add life to your vertical garden whether it is inside your house or outside.

Conclusion

Vertical gardens are perfect for people who live in urban areas and therefore might have less room for gardening.

They are also ideal for people who want to grow their own produce and are skeptical about the nutritional value of the fruits and vegetables sold in the market.

This book is a beginner's guide for all the people who want green walls flourishing in their houses allowing them to breathe in clean and fresh air.

Read this book and make use of all the tips and ideas compiled in it and witness a piece of art growing and unraveling on the walls of your house.

Now go out there and start your very own vertical garden!

About The Author

Tom Ford is an expert at everything related to leaves, trees, flowers and pretty much everything that grows in the moist aromatic soil.

He has been gardening since the age of six when he assisted his grandmother in taking care of her vegetable garden.

Since then he has pursued a career in horticulture and has become a recognizable authority providing his expertise and sharing this passion with others.

Check Out These Books

The Perfect Compost Plan

Container Gardening Made Simple

Enjoy this book?

Please leave a review below and let us know what you liked about this book by clicking on the Amazon image below.

and click on Digital Orders.

The above link directs to Amazon.com. Please change the .com to your own country extension.

Printed in the USA
CPSIA information can be obtained
at www.ICGtesting.com
LVHW050234100124
768593LV00037BC/972